Another Word for Hunger

Sundress Publications • Knoxville, TN

Editor: Sherrel McLafferty
Managing Editor: Tennison Black
Editorial Assistant: Kanika Lawton
Editorial Interns: Kaylee Young-Eun Jeong, Robin LaMer Rahija,
Eden Stiger, Max Stone, and Nicole Bethune Winters

Colophon: This book is set in EB Garamond
Cover Art: "Dream Girl" by Zoobia Asghar
Cover Design: Kristin Ton
Book Design: Sherrel McLafferty

Another Word for Hunger

Heather Bartlett

Acknowledgements

Many thanks to the following publications in which versions of these poems first appeared:

Barrow Street: "This is What We Made"
Carolina Quarterly: "Ars[on] Poetica: Letter After" and "Semiotics"
Connotation Press: "Go Like This" and "Morningsong"
Driftwood: "This is Not About the Birds"
Evening Street Review: "Lexapro, 10mg"
The Fiddlehead: "Etymology" and "Fall"
Lambda Literary: "Eve"
The Nervous Breakdown: "Perseids, August"
Nimrod International Journal: "We Return to Ritual"
Ninth Letter: "red | wolf"
Phoebe: "Mockingbird," "Tonight I Am"
Poem Memoir Story: "When I Was a Boy"
Poet Lore: "It Starts Like This"
Prime Number Magazine: "Mercy" and "She Tries to Teach Me the Principle of Non-Attachment"
Redivider: "These Lines"
RHINO: "That is Not My Name"
Rise Up Review: "Resistance"
Quarterly West: "Malapropism"

Contents

three

"There are things lovely and dangerous still."
—June Jordan

red | wolf

(I haven't eaten
        for days) this
is my penance:

the sound of your knuckle
        against the metal doorframe
(if I failed to answer
        would you turn away
or would you keep)
        knocking (I hear you)
until I invited you in

(I see) the long shadow of
        your body like a whip
(come closer so I can
        feel you) dancing
in the sunlight (are you real
        are you) dressed and
ready (for me)

this is the root of hunger:
        reaching for the thick slice
of your cheek (flushing
        against my hand)
is this meant for me
        to take (will you come)
in to swim inside
        my hollow body
(will you come) you
        taste like me.

one

How to Weed the Garden

The calendar tells me today
is a Tuesday. I continue to cross

off the days, but what good is an X
when there is no countdown?

I used to leave
sticky notes on doorknobs:

*Turn off the coffee pot. But first
make more. Make time*

*for to-go cups and disposable lids and
one more walk through the garden.*

What good is a doorknob?
How many afternoons

have I been wearing this sweater, pulling
at its pills and rolling

to the next episode: on this show
it is always night and

there are sirens everywhere.
I haven't lifted the blinds

in six days. Maybe seven.
This kind of counting

will make you weep. This kind
of weeping will dry you up.

Look at these hard hands,
at the hard ground. Even the soil

is tired of waiting. It's not
that I can't wait a little longer;

it's the dandelions, those dumb flowers
poking through the dirt.

These Lines

are not linear   look:
this line is where you come out

this line is also tomorrow
tomorrow is also the girl

from yesterday
this is what she says:

your memories are also
my memories wrapped

in silk and sewn
into the seams   remember

bare legs   black lace   this
is what boys like: stay

still   breathe in
like you need

lifting like you are
too much smoke

and not enough   this
is what you get: the boy

slides closer   he always
slides   the girl

from yesterday makes
eye contact   breaks

contact   look:
your finger is on the zipper

instead of the collar
instead of the bone

this is what you get:
stay still   breathe in like

you are too much   this
is what she says:

these lines are also
my body   your body

is on fire

Malapropism

I never learned to read skeletons the way my mother did: follow the line of three stars with your eyes, she said, keep moving up, and up, until you find it, the shoulder bone, and from here you can point the arrow. See? I was five, maybe six. She lifted my arm and pointed my hand toward the sky. I wanted to see. I squinted. Closed one eye at a time. Asked her to show me again. Again. But I could not see it. That night, my mother stood on my twin bed and stuck glowing paper stars to the ceiling, careful to recreate the pattern so I would remember: a bright line, five stars to make the flexed curve of a bow.

Or: if I tattoo this skeleton into my flesh, will it change the way I see the sky.

Or: this constellation will never survive my brutal body.

Etymology

Aren't we obsessed
with origins. The grief
consuming those red
woods began with the old
English *wilde fyr*
with a firework
or downed power line
or discarded cigarette.
As soon as it reaches
the property line
we will start
tracing its history. Each
investigation begins with
intent. This is how
we justify the instinct
to flee. Fire
used to mean lightning
used to mean lightning rod
used to mean glass
in the sand. What was wild

was our desire

to hold it. If Eve

had struck a match

in the Garden,

which would have burned

first—his ribs or

her hair or

our impulse to touch?

What Eve Knew

This is not my first
time. I was always out

of breath always
keeping count. Listen,

in the beginning it came
slowly, an itch

under my foot, stinging
between my legs,

dryness in my mouth
until I could only taste

skin. Call it
practice or preparation

or undoing. It doesn't matter.
The next time

I found the residue
on my pillowcase

thick and dark like blood
from my nose. I touched it,

rubbed it between my fingers,
tasted it and waited

for it to come again.
It came.

Swept in through a crack
in the window, didn't even hover

above me, just went
straight for my mouth.

It Starts Like This

She calls and asks
if you've settled in. You know

she means, are you ever
coming home. Tell her

you've joined a book club.
Bought a yoga mat. Tell her

the days here
are five minutes longer

and five minutes feels like
another to do list:

Hang up the laundry.
Hang up the phone.

Write a ~~poem~~ letter.
Learn a new

language. Remember
this word — *brûler*.

Then, it's everything all over
again: Mornings.

Putting on your socks
before getting out of bed.

Spilling the sugar.
Sweeping the sugar. Practicing

in the mirror, raised
eyebrow, chin tuck. Hanging up.

Watching that movie
about the woman

who buys the house
with the built-in bunker.

Making your own
in your claw foot

tub. Taking two
bunker baths a day

because wet skin feels
like a fire suit.

Blessing

"Listen to what the water says." –Sam Hamill

Tell me how the blessing works.
I reach my hands
into the water and—
what about the man
who spat at our feet and called it
the cure? There it is,
he said, lick it up.

Tell me again
how the prayer goes. Words won't
stick with me long enough
to be repeated. But I think
it starts with
because. Blessing is another word
for grief. Tell me

how to hold my hands. I cup them
full of cold water and
what? Lift them to my lips?
This can't be right.
Because a blessing is a story.

Tell me one about the mouth.
Because I can't feel my fingers,
but I remember counting
the stairs we climbed to get here:
forty-two steps, two
stories. In this one,

I haven't sipped.
I haven't prayed.

I haven't felt another person's skin
in months. Here it is:
Empty hand. Icy water.

Resistance

Sure, you want to create
a space to resist,
to form yourself whole at its center

& stay there, but where I
come from, you can't
escape tradition: stand near

a man, slouch & sit
on his knee, but don't crease
the fabric. *Be Nice.*

   (this is always present tense)

Let's say you ask for something — more ice
or a spoon — & the waiter teases
only if you say pretty please. It's

only after you say the words & eat
with the prettyplease spoon, that you stare
at the table and feel hot recognition rise

into your neck. This is what he sees:
a girl enters
a room alone. She isn't

looking at other men. She must need care.
No one seems to tire
of this. Not even your own sense

of self & space can
stop it in real time. You can't erase
the way your body reads. See:
> even your mother says, *what is
> so wrong with being nice?*

That Kind of Hunger

In my young-girl body, still
          bony and flat chested, it was easy enough

to play the prince: keep her
          waiting, climb the branches, pluck

the closest berry (do not
          bite it) wait for her

to beg. But she was in it for the curse:
          that kind of hunger could turn

the earth to black water, sin
          to swan, breath to stone, stone

to sleep. My prince-body knew
          what to do: watch her

watch me, trace the soft lines
          of her body (do not

touch). But dusk would come before
          I could save her. Fairy tales

stop long before the prince
          becomes the beggar, the body

becomes her own, swelling and starving.
          How could we know

what it meant when they cut down
          the tree and burned the blossoms.

How could we leave
      the roots to shrivel beneath us.

We didn't know we couldn't harvest
      fruit from ash.

Stand Here, You Said, and Wait
after Rene Magritte's "The Lovers," 1928

Here has become a place we steal
    away to: hand & hip &
breath against neck. Looking
    but not looking
we loan each small part
    as if the offering of fingertips,
leaning of a shoulder blade,
    lending of a collarbone,
could be an act
    of contrition. It is the giving
back we regret most. We are
    voyeurs watching as we move
around ourselves, taking in
    what is not shown
& aren't we amazed
    how close this holding
back has brought us. Here
    we are almost
what we'd hoped for:
    bound & tied & wanting
like two masked lovers, blind
    to touch, hoping to feel
through thick cotton, moving
    into each other anyway.

Tonight I Am

I slip into other identities
the ways she slips
into terry cloth shorts.
I watch her

crouch and turn
sliding them over her small
legs and adjusting them
as she pivots.
Tonight I am

someone else—
the neighbor
across the hall who wonders
why our lights are never on,
who keeps a close eye
out the peephole for a glimpse
of petite brunette. For a moment

I am the missing child
from the evening news,
curled up in a small bed waiting
to be found. I am the mother
who lost the child. I am the reporter
with the microphone saying,
"if" and "return." I am

my lover, watching me
from across the room.

Lexapro, 10mg
for the treatment of severe depression or mild anxiety disorder

What does it feel like?

She is always asking
in the same way
and every week
I tell her
I'm dying.

When my hands are numb
I shake them
clench them and
press them against my teeth.

What happens next?

When the vertigo starts
I move to the stairs,
try to walk down them
without falling, one hand
against the wall.
I'm dying.

Have you been writing?

I've been dreaming of a woman.
She puts one hand
behind my head
and pulls. She puts
her lips over mine

and inhales
every word.
She chews them
swallows them
and smiles.

Have you been writing?

This woman is stealing
everything I have left:

the smell of sweat
on my pillow. A fistful
of glass beads
and a book at the end
of the bed.

How does it start?

When my hands
are numb I will spill
the beads onto the floor
like water.

Morningsong

What was it that kept us
    before all this giving up:

the color of the room
    when the sky is about to turn to storm
        or early morning

& my fingers cannot trace your form
    in the dark

when the kettle no longer whistles
    & boiling water
        splinters the thin glass

when I open the door
    & the light from the porch is enough

to show the deliberate & empty space
    our bodies have given up
        while the morning breaks & you

are not yet awake to say
    we wanted this

Jerusalem Hill

from here we can see
everything   the prison
and surrounding
wire mesh fence
the rusted gates to the city
the stain the flood left
along Church Street

eventually we will learn
to tell this story
with a soundtrack
of affirmations   yes
we wanted to stay
we wanted to
rebuild   we'll tell it
with a photo
of the large elm
that met us
at the end of the road
we'll say we came here

so we could walk down
to the creek and splash
our faces with fresh water
we'll say we came
to bury our toes into the earth
where the farmhouse used to be
where we swung as kids
on the thick rope under
the elm   but this

was all long before you
and me and the rope swing
is just a story I've told
ever since I learned
a girl is expected
to have stories

Second Place

What is the line from
that folk song I loved

as a teen. What is the name
for the kind of bee

that doesn't sting. It should be
so easy. Like my grandmother's

old phone number. I know
I know this. I can hear the music.

See the bee's fuzzy coat.
Feel the receiver buttons

against my cheek. But
nothing else. I try

to call up the name for this.
I call my mother instead.

You're just foggy, she says.
This isn't the word

I'm looking for
but it will do. Remember,

she says, the pi contest.
And I do:

Thirteen, sitting at a metal desk
in the middle of a circle of desks.

My turn. I had been memorizing
for weeks *3.14159*

I spun my hand in small circles
with each cluster of digits *26535*

My math teacher seemed to be holding
her breath *89793*

— there's more. I know
there's more.

And you won!
my mother says. But I didn't win.

A boy named Kenny beat me
by five digits *32384*

You remember, my mother says.
And I do:

the smell of grass and sweat and
all those bees swarming the window.

Mercy

Take this she says—

        voice low, like a child

                learning how to pitch

her cries, a mother holding

        back, a woman

                weighted under another—hold

her face close to

        yours. Closer. Breathe

                soap & lipstick. Close

your eyes. Move them

        side to side against

                the lids. *Take it*. Feel it

pulsing in your mouth

        like an electric bassline.

                Is it enough to be

ready? Take her

        cold hands, rub

                yourself into them.

That Is Not My Name

When I close my eyes there's a brass handle
but in my hand there's only

a bobby pin. I never learned
how to pick locks. How to enter

a room without making a sound.
The sound of stealing is much

like when you say *Darling*
but that is not my name. I only learned

how to turn the deadbolt, to wedge
the board under the knob so the door

couldn't be opened from the outside.
When I close my eyes

someone is knocking. I never learned
how to code switch. The right word

when someone expects return.
How do I let myself

out if the handle will not move?
If the answer is the same

in any language? *Oh,*
Darling. That is not my hand.

This is not my mouth. There must be
another word for this.

Ars[on] Poetica

What they won't tell you
is there was nothing else left
to burn. The first time
we prayed, she pressed
her hand against my ribs:

thumb first, then
index finger, then
the rest. It was not
for mercy;

it was for electricity
enough to raise
the fine hair from her arms
thumb, index, press
a static charge to every
press. No body
without its own current.
I'm still waiting for this
to pass through me. You see,

the danger was never
the fire
or the hand. It doesn't matter
that we could never
go back; they will weep
anyway. This is how it spreads,
love after

destruction. They will tell you
I'm guilty:
soaked each word

with gasoline, lit
the match, watched one catch
and ignite the next until
no silhouette could stand out against
the flame.

Haven't you ever
read by the glow of bone
turning to ash?

two

This Body Is Temporary

haven't you already tried
to suck marrow
from stone
the salt wet stain
of old rain
all that is left to taste?

Preparations

& here is the birthmark
above my left ear
that mother calls *beauty*
as she brushes my damp hair
holding up the loose strands
so they can't drip
& she tells me
someday I will learn
what it means to want more
woman she says
still brushing
sorry when she hits
a knot and I pull
my head forward
stay still

Mother(s)

Isn't this what you really wanted
more: a tiny fist, a reason
to sew a pocket.

Remember What She Told You

didn't you see me
hands cupped and

ready to catch
what you let

drop

       face
       waist
       yes
       one used match
       after another

If Early in the Morning

a crack in the ceiling
    bends down the wall
behind the bed
    splitting us like twins
we clutch at corners
    and shield our eyes

but the door is still
    slightly open
bleeding yellow light
    onto our faces—

Remember What Comes Next

—the sound of a belt
buckle falling
from chair
to carpet.

As a Girl

it's like the way
our muscles ache
from preparing
instead of starting

like the way
the body mistakes
thirst for famine

I won't say your name
but I'll write it

This Is What You Get

every sound
is something else — a whisper
is a warning
is a craving — but the walls
still recognize the thud
of our bones tossed
upon the bed.

Making the Bed

what good are these bones
if not
for breaking
for bending & knocking
against new joints
here   a shoulder blade
finds its place
inside the hollow
curve of an elbow

When I Was a Boy

, but what about
    the bones we collected
& buried,

the bowl of broken
    pencils under the bed—

this was how we prayed
    with the snap
of yellow & lead.

three

This Is What the Fire Meant

All of us. Music
from a car radio
& drinks in plastic cups.
It was not

sex. It meant
not going home
even if home
was warm & safe
& in walking distance.

Let me be clear:
it was not sex.
It meant closing
my eyes, warming
my fingers, feet, belly.

Two girls on one flat stone
meant a reason to slide
my jeans, my legs, my
self further toward
the edge. It meant
balancing with one leg
stretched out to the side.
In the morning,

when we were all waking,
when cars pulled away
& the pit offered
only smoke,

it meant
finding another way
to keep warm.

In Some Way We Are Always Leaving Each Other

she told me to be with a man
she told me

it was a test
the fading imprint of a body

in the mattress   the short cry
& pinch   the hard

& pulling grasp
so tight I think this

is the last one
we are always leaving

clothes piled on the floor
robes bought & never

worn   bruised bed corners
pillowcases drenched

with thirst
we leave & return

tired & shaking
before we turn

to sleep   she pulls
my body under hers

& we are leaving each
other even now   lying

tangled & breathless
pulling the wrinkled sheet

up over us

Eve

There you were:
      a sliver in the pink of my palm

you were the frayed wood
      dangling from the table you were

the wrinkled lines inside my fist
      you followed me

up the metal stairs &
      into the warm kitchen you

lit the burner & boiled the water
      you were the steam &

my breath on the cold pane turning
      to ice on the other side

of thick glass you broke
      through & sat on my chest

as I sang shivering & barefoot
      on the cold floor you were

the sweet bloody hole when I pulled
      the sliver out.

Evensong

It should not surprise you
that contrition makes me
uncomfortable. Like confession,

shedding a layer of sin
in order to be saved. I confess
I never wanted forgiveness

I just loved the idea of taking
turns. Confess. Forgive. First
I will be the sinner—

*I didn't mean to do it. I only
wanted you to say
not yet.* And now you—

forgive me. We could
keep this up all night. My turn,
your turn, swapping remorse for

redemption. But in the morning,
when we emerge, purged and reborn,
every face looks like you.

I Spy

One of my loves
took a walk through town
in silver sneakers. One
of my loves took selfies
in stage costumes. I click
through their lives
from a safe distance. I do everything
from a safe distance. Tonight
I'm spying on the woman
I couldn't love back.
Now I miss her
like cappuccinos and airplane seats.
I miss her hands
but they are not
her hands. They are
the hands from the leather glove
ad that pops up every time
I log in. We remember everything
new in lockdown. Which is to say,
we remember only what we have
made up in the dark. This woman's
face is lighting up
my screen. My love. Her hands,
her hands are open.
I click to like. I click to reply.
The cursor blinks. I can't remember
what I wanted to say.

Perseids, August

We are both outside
waiting past midnight for the meteor
shower that neither of us
can see.

Over the phone
in the dark, we tell
stories of our day—

a short walk across
the small bridge and
through the empty
parking lot, an hour
of writing and deleting lines
about your body, the bitter
smell outside a downtown
coffee house, a longer walk
home, a glimpse
of you, but
it wasn't you,
crossing the street—

until we both
go quiet in searching, letting
our eyes adjust to the dark,
waiting for something
to streak across the sky.

Fall

those were the nights
when we stood in the street

& held our demands up
over our heads. when we held

our bodies up with nothing
more than suspenders & tape.

when we would have done anything
to feel what they felt. when you said

there was no relief.
when the streetlight

was suddenly brilliant
before going out

& it was so dark you thought
you couldn't breathe.

when the neighbor's house
was burglarized & we

didn't yet know the sound
of firecrackers or flares

was actually the blast
of a gun. when nothing

lit up the sky. when we learned
the language of urgency

too late. if it's relief you want
start looking with your hands.

Semiotics

What words did she write
    in your palm. Did you lick
the bitter ink or let it smear
    inside your pocket.

This is what you wanted:
    pins & needles, bite
marks, stained & calloused
    fingertips, the still wet

scent of her mouth inside
    your fist. She said
you can believe something
    by touching it

but even against this
    hot shadow, you tremble.
Did you know these fingers
    would betray you?

How far can you reach before
    pulling back, before her words
melt with sweat, before
    you say enough. Look:

fireflies are circling the flames
    & you can't tell
flightless embers from the deliberate
    patterns of bugs.

Go Like This

"And I want it still for me here now as I lie in the blue-black of this aloneness thirsting for love more than I ever thought I could." —Lorrie Moore

Let the word roll over
in your mouth.

It feels like
memorizing lines of numbers

or verse, like falling into white heat, like
biting your lip. She wants you

to ask a question — no — she wants
an answer. Like this:

*the clouds tonight are mercury-quilted
and wrapping us in warm rain.*

She tells you she likes the idea of something
to believe in. She has a way

of reaching around you
so all night you will be searching

for more of that scent. Stitch your own
into her dress. Write a letter

that's only for you. Start
like this: *I no longer believe*

in black and white. Carry it with you
in the blue-black dark. But watch

where you step;
the leaves have covered the sidewalk

and now this way looks the same
as the sky. You want to go—

wait — like this: the crisp edge
of paper splits you open.

Mockingbird

I wanted to scoop myself out
to make room
for you   (who wouldn't rather be
        the house
        than the tenant) you wanted

to hide inside this wax cavern
to sing without
being seen.

Like this: my belly becomes
a vacancy song. My chest
a ready nest of ribs
and mud   (remember
        the way every move
        made a sound
        made an echo made
        you shudder) This body

is a cacophony of call
and recall: I will wait. *I will*
        break. I want you. *I want you*
        to leave

when every voice is
someone else   (you laughing)
and every move is   (bone against)
stone

        this body
        is willing but the walls
        are sinking.

The mockingbird
sings   *grief* but what I said
                   was *relief*. Please

                   get out.

Notes on Coming Out

My mother says
boys don't wear ruffles

and girls don't wear
tool belts. She will never

understand my desire
to build things. Shelves. Tables.

Stained wood porches. Even this
page. This corner. This

white edge was folded
by my own careful hands.

When was the last time
I tried to act like a girl.

Tried to sing the right words
or push the right button.

I tell her about yesterday.
Stuck in the elevator

with the boy with the toy
gun. How he yelled bang!

as the doors closed.
I tell her

it's not about
tool belts or how long

I can hold
my breath. It's about

preservation. Floorboards.
Steps. These refurbished

spindles. I want to keep
building stairways.

I want more
worthy exits. Take my hand,

I should have told the boy.
Take my pulse.

But please.
Don't shoot me.

New Year

by now the balloons
have sunken to eye level

& you say
that's how this works

no   not say   said
yesterday rings in our ears

our resolve still sticky
on our tongues

we were   we are
plucking paper promises

from a basket & stuffing them
into our pockets

throwing noisemakers & cardboard
hats onto the heap

there is still an inch left
to the sparkler

I can see my fingers but
the room & the baskets & your body

are already gone to the dark
even my wrist is lost

as the spark burns down
yesterday is erasing us

the old year spills
off the steps into the parking lot

while we said
no   we sang

remember this
remember this

She Tries to Teach Me the Principle of Non-Attachment

Like slicing the string, she says, eyes half-closed, *and catching it.*
We're standing socked feet on her vinyl floor — cheek to cheek

and leaning against each other. We play a game: *Tell me*
I say, and she whispers — tonight

it's her turn — *a body is a blade.* We light candles
and watch them color the room fog and orange.

Tell me I say, and she pulls us onto the blanket
on the floor. We're eye to eye now

trying not to blink, both that sepia hue
spilling down into coarse fabric. The small stone Buddha

watches us, knees bent, arm draped over leg,
wrist down, flashing his toothless smile. We turn

away from him, legs wrapped together. The light
flickers. *Tell me.* A blade, a finger falls. I blink.

Skin

Touch me here
       where I used to feel
the static crease &
       split the sting
of a needle pierced
       through & pulling
the stitch after you
       put me back
together. Parts of me
       are dead. Touch me
here. Feel it raised
       and slightly rougher
than the living.

& Bones

Did she jump.
Did she do it

right. In her version,
there is a price

for gravity. Thin
fingernails score

miniature moons
into her palms,

tiny half crests or
recurring Cs:

*Cutting. Crumbling. Countless.
Common.* Watch her

fall back over front over
the wall. In this version,

there's still time
for rearranging the fragments

into a new shape.
Here she is

cobbled together
from clay and cracked

buttons, almost the color
of metal. Tell me

how stitching open wounds
heals anything.

We Return to Ritual

to the graveyard we hunted
     as girls
spreading paper rolls
     across the stones
like sheets over corpses
     rubbing thick chalk back
and forth to raise
     words from the dead

the ritual was in the reveal
     we held our breaths
while letters became faces
     numbers became bodies
we pressed paper to muddy earth
     wanting to feel
more than ourselves we
     were so close

Nectar

I am watching her make her way back
to bed. It's been a long day of trying

not to name the things
we cannot have, and now we're stripped

of anything that was left. She pushes
her fingers into my hair, guides

mine to her soft belly. She wears
her thirst like scars,

faded but smooth to touch. This one
is for when I didn't let her fuck me

when she was sorry; this
is for when I did. This

is for when I left her
to sweep up the spider webs

alone. We're almost
out of blank space. I am watching her

drink this in, cup it in her hands, sip
and swallow, handful

after handful filling her
from the bottom up.

This Is What We Made

As told by X

A man wants to write the story
of us. *What really happened?* Only
he doesn't want to know
what really happened—

At night she wrapped me
in the bed sheets'
folded edges, tucked
the corners under
my feet, like the way
the young hospice nurse
delicately bound
her mother's body.
The nights were always
for holding on.
She held herself
above me, arched her back.
She told me
to close my eyes. She told me
we were falling
into something

—he only wants to know
how she said it.

As told by Ex

A man wants to write
the story of us.
It's simple—

        I took
what she gave:
shoulder blade, hip
bone. I drank in bits
of her breath, the smell
of her neck
after a day at work.
She gave them
one at a time, slowly
breathing a little harder
each time I took. I could take
and take until my hands
were full of her
until she was lying
arms and legs spread
empty on the bed.

The Day After That

These sudden branches
are so like your arms, this
cold dirt so like
your body. Please

don't mistake me; this is not
an insult. What I mean to say

is I can't find a foothold
to start my climb, a limb
thick enough to bear the weight
of all our do-overs—

touch this, pinch,
etch, push back and
release. Did you
carve my initials
into this bark?

I'm reading your knots,
your not yets.
Not even skin
can distinguish
departure from return—

in this dark, my bare arm
is the same color
as the tree; only passing
headlights interrupt
this closeness.
This is when I know
it's time

to dig. What I mean to say is
I was aiming
in the wrong direction.

This Is Not About the Birds

the crows have come
back   so many black wings
among the branches
that I can't remember
when the leaves fell
away   before you said
no I said
this is not about
the way things drop

this is not about
the birds   you said
the word for this
kind of flight
is *invitation*   to the crows

a woman's open hand looks
like a question
to the crows   her body
is thicker
than its shadow   no

this is not a metaphor
the right word
is *invasion*   a woman
opens her hand
to block   her body
weeps   now they all want
a turn at the flesh   no
the crows are not perched
in waiting   you know
the word for this

Red Eye

/ /

We're sitting alone at the back
of the plane, three rows
from the emergency exit.
The flight attendant offers me
water. My lover
offers me headphones. *Sleep*
she says and opens her book.

/ /

Will you ever come back? my mother asks
when I tell her I love
a woman.

/ /

We are making a list
of things we've witnessed:

a flock of birds rising
and falling together,
a handful of glass, white
sheets draped over
a woman's dead body.

/ /

My mother is pushing away
her wine glass, fingertip to stem.

She is daring me
to catch it.

Will you ever come back?

/ /

The cabin is dark. My tray table
shakes. We'll be landing
soon. *Almost* my lover says
and puts her hand on my leg.
The city is coming into focus
below us — street lights and rooftops,

the tall red beacons outside
the airport. *Yes*
I say and lean against the window.
Yes and she takes her hand away.

Everything We Knew Yesterday

is a lie — the lone

lily wrapped in damp

paper & left

balancing on the doorknob

did not open

for you. It was not

pink but burnt

orange & wilting.

It was not

the sound of rain; it was

the boy running

toward you.

The door

would not stay

shut. The window

would not crack.

Our voices did not

carry; they couldn't hear

a thing. The first time

was not the first

but the last

time you ever

felt so—

Dear Eve

the body knows two things:
how to recognize itself in the dark
& when to beg for more.
you already know how to move

& recognize yourself in the dark.
tonight you are the boy.
you already know every move,
every snap fastening this closed.

tonight you are the boy
which means everything is backwards.
every move is a snap. fasten this closed
so no one can see you fully.

everything is backwards, which means
you can feel every inch
but no one can see you fully.
you know what this means.

you can feel. every inch
of your body is contracting.
you know what this means.
everything is about to speed up.

your body is a contract with the living.
today you are the girl.
everything is about to speed up
& every word is a tourniquet.

today you are yourself.
let the blood flow back into your hand.

every word is a turn.
where do we go from here:
back into your hand.
the body knows
we can go anywhere from here
please

Notes

"Resistance" is an "anagram/word scramble" poem, a form I adopted from Donna Masini, who adopted it from Terrence Hayes.

"That is Not My Name" is after Max Ritvo's poem "The Hope Chest."

"Stand Here, You Said, And Wait" is a somewhat ekphrastic poem after Rene Magritte's The Lovers, 1928.

The cycle of poems in the second section, comprised of titles and endings, came out of an exploration of the relationships between beginnings and endings, before and after, and text and white space.

"Go Like This" is after Lorrie Moore's short story of the same title, which appears in her collection, Self-Help.

"Fall" is after Jan Heller Levi's poem, "That Was the Fall."

"The Day After That" is after Priscilla Becker's poem, "If You Think It Takes Longer."

Thank You

To Sherrel McLafferty, Tennison S. Black, Erin Elizabeth Smith, and all the editors, readers, and designers at Sundress Publications for seeing and fostering the power in this collection;

to my brilliant teachers, Donna Masini, Jan Heller Levi, and Mary J. Mahoney for every word;

to Maggie Smith for helping me break these poems open;

to my writing family, especially Chelsea Bunn, Sara Rempe, Katie Marks, Amy Monticello, Kati Ahern, Tyler Bradway, Cori McKenzie, and Michael Turner for carrying pieces of this with me;

to the English Department at SUNY Cortland for your support and cheerleading;

to my students for always surprising me;

to Marnie Waxman for every reminder;

to Gillian Frew for every nudge;

to Andrea Rosati for seeing me;

to Jaime Warburton for recognizing me;

to my sister, Holly Thompson, for always being my person;

to my mom, dad, and family for giving me everything I needed to find all these versions of myself;

to everyone who has held me up and pushed me through;

to everyone who has paved this way;

and to anyone who follows me in:

thank you.

About the Author

Heather Bartlett is a poet, writer, and professor. Her poetry and prose can be found in print and online in journals such as *Barrow Street, Lambda Literary, Ninth Letter, Quarterly West, RHINO Poetry, Poet Lore*, and others. She holds an MFA in Poetry from Hunter College and teaches creative writing and writing studies at the State University of New York at Cortland. She is the founding editor of the online literary magazine *Hoxie Gorge Review*. She writes in coffee shops in New York and Edinburgh, Scotland.

Find more of her work at heatherbartlett.com.

Other Sundress Titles

Little Houses
Athena Nassar
$16.00

Where My Umbilical is Buried
Amanda Galvan Huynh
$12.99

In Stories We Thunder
V. Ruiz
$12.99

the Colored page
Matthew E. Henry
$12.99

Slack Tongue City
Mackenzie Berry
$12.99

Year of the Unicorn Kidz
jason b. crawford
$12.99

Sweetbitter
Stacey Balkun
$12.99

Something Dark to Shine In
Inès Pujos
$12.99

Cosmobiological: Stories
Jilly Dreadful
$16.99

Slaughter the One Bird
Kimberly Ann Priest
$12.99

The Valley
Esteban Rodriguez
$12.99

What Nothing
Anna Meister
$12.99

CPSIA information can be obtained
at www.ICGtesting.com
Printed in the USA
JSHW080930020623
42592JS00005B/24